D0589152

A Song for Hāna
&
the Spirit of Lehoʻula

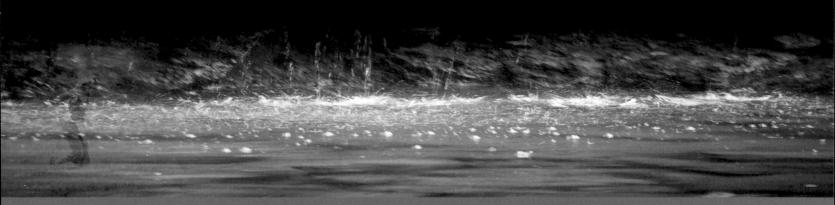

To Kathy

Morning she searched the field
All day the kitchen table
blazed with flowers

Library of Congress Control Number: 2007900189
ISBN 978-0-9791743-2-2
Copyright © 2007 George D. Kinder

All rights reserved. No part of this book may be reproduced or transmitted in any form or by any means, electronic or mechanical, including photocopying, recording or by any information storage and retrieval system, without written permission from the author, except for the inclusion of brief quotations for review.

Some words and definitions used by permission from *Hawaiian Dictionary* by Pukui and Elbert © 1986 University of Hawaii Press

Printed in the United States of America on acid-free paper and meets NISO standards for permanence and durability.

Serenity Point Press
business@serenitypoint.org
www.serenitypoint.org

To My Readers

Although I wrote *A Song for Hāna & the Spirit of Leho'ula* as an attempt to save the coastal land in Hāna from development, the book was never intended to be primarily about the saving of that land. It is also about the larger environment, where landscapes of ocean, earth and air are threatened constantly by human encroachments. When the poem speaks of Hāna it is about that sacred place, 'the last Hawaiian place,' and it is about the earth. The poem, as metaphor, speaks though to still larger ground. It speaks to the terrain just inside our skin, the landscape of our spirit, the place in which our own ground crumbles beneath us, our own swirling seas threaten to devour us. More than anything, it is a poem about this inner landscape, how we threaten it, how we fall asleep to it, and how by waking up our inner world we save the land around us.

A Song for Hāna is a poem of my own daily journey for many years across these landscapes, searching for the present moment, trying to understand what it means not to get lost, to face (as part of that) my own anxieties and concerns, and to undertake, for hours a day, a spiritual practice that took me deeper and deeper into the landscapes of Hāna and of myself.

Part of my work involved getting to know the history and stories of the ancient ones, the ancestors of the Hawaiian people who walked the same stretch of coast before me, and to speak to them in my own way. Humbled by the experience of finding a personal connection with them, and a mutual love of the land and its spirit, I knew no way to talk of the experiences I found other than to personify the spirits that I conversed with in the forms of ancient Hawaii. I truly hope that, as a man originating in a different culture, I have offended no one. What I learned felt universal, applicable to all cultures, and urgent to tell.

The six chapters are organized both as a physical and as a spiritual journey. To guide you on this journey, I've used photographs of the landscape and scans of local vegetation. All images were taken along this single mile of Hawaiian coast. I've also employed several poetic forms. There are poems, prose poems and prose pieces. The prose pieces are usually meant as transitions to move the action of the story. The shorter poems are designed to capture a momentary experience. Longer poems elaborate on the meaning of experiences described in the narrative. The longest narrative poems expand upon the journey's meaning and occupy much of the dialogue between the spirits of Pele, Leho'ula and myself.

I invite you to explore the images and poetry in whatever way feels natural to you. Visually, each two-page spread is a moment in time. Just as every moment is different from every other, so each spread is meant to be different. Sometimes words so intermingle with the life of the earth or the life of the sea that it takes some effort to discern them. This is also as it is meant to be. You may wish to survey the landscape page-by-page from above, alighting on a particular poem that draws you with its shape or its placement or its connection with an image. Or perhaps you will wish to start from the beginning of the book and read straight through. *A Song for Hāna* invites many readings, and I am grateful for them all.

Finally, while this book employs endangered Hāna as metaphor for the earth, and for our eroding inner landscapes, I am deeply concerned with the threat development poses to Hāna the place, and am committed to preserving this sacred coast, and to supporting Hawaiian culture. Given this commitment, I thought for a long time about the share of the profits that will go to Hāna and its people. I considered ten percent because of the spiritual tradition of tithing. But it did not feel nearly enough. I then considered one-hundred percent, because I want to save the land and give back to Hāna and its traditional culture in every way I can. But I realized that if I donated one-hundred percent of the profits, I could not then afford to give nearly the amount of time or energy that I would like to support these causes. So I settled on at least fifty percent of the profits and much time and energy. This feels like a gift in balance, and I am happy to have you join with me in its giving. At the back of this volume are lists of organizations and people who have contributed much to Hāna or to this book.

With aloha from Hāna,

George Kinder

Contents

MY OCCUPATION:
LISTENER TO THE LAND

This is a dangerous job
Watching moments at Lehoʻula
Dangerous as fishing on the tempestuous seas

Trees and rocks fall
from the cliffs of Ka iwi o Pele

Riptides tear
Storms appear

When it's clear
sun scorches the sand

Each of these elements
has been drawn to Lehoʻula
How could I not come?

The Gate to the Garden

In which I wrestle with my tasks and responsibilities and the daily news, and am called by the sea, by the wind, by Lehoʻula to enter the pastures and do the spiritual work that is Hāna.

Tracing Nature's delicate Lines across the Page

I plod along the surface of things
Walking on the planks of my deck
Reading the daily news

Underneath, I am urgent
Breathless to discover
how to break through
how to reveal what is true

Stopping, I listen
Quiet as earth
Concentrated as the eye

of a storm

I
Again and again the wind
with inarticulate roar
falls awkwardly against me
with its news

What urgent message does it carry
that keeps the arms of the banyan reaching
and the ocean raging?

II
All those wiggles in the waves
speak a secret language:

Their current sparks my fingers;
They dance along the sockets
of my spine, telegraphing,
an ancient code

What is it you have to tell me
this chill winter day?

III
My body slapped by a banyan leaf
Fear rushes up my spine
I hear voices from behind
But it is the ocean talking.

I was deep in a reverie of fields, immobile trees
and hills, which dotted the landscape,
when the sea spoke to me

I was so stunned
I can not recall
what it said.

I observe the dance
of ironwood trees in morning air
Cap of my pen in my lips
Dark clouds overhead
Bulls graze in front of me
Kitchen sounds come from inside
I wonder how to make meaning of it
The sky opens, releases
Water pours

Thousands of drops pass my eyes in a moment
Minah birds cry out
        white and black wings beating
I love the birds, but oh how I long to live
in each drop of rain as it passes

Across the ocean I spy snow
on Mauna Kea's peak

Drops of rain splatter my ink
Winds gather about me
A rainbow appears
The ocean roars below

I hover over a tablet
and write all that I know

I live on the edge of a garden,
a museum of all that is present
and all that has passed away:
Three pastures
and then the great God of a hill
Ka iwi o Pele with its wild rusty skirts
Falling down to Leho'ula

I long for deeper peace
Surely the answer lies here
In the moments, in the garden

Long before the sun finds its winding way
out of the star-strewn water
I walk through the wooden gate
rusted with summer salt
yearning for Leho'ula

Each morning I walk out into the sky
and cry out, tell me your meaning!

The sun, without saying a word
rises from its ocean bed
and spreads a tapestry
from Ka'uiki to Ka iwi o Pele

I walk carefully
Passing coconut fronds
and bull droppings
in standing clumps
of dew grass

Cross the field
to the trail
fishermen use

With their families
and their dogs
Gear piled high
in pick-up trucks

Down to the lava
at ocean's edge—
Waipama.

At the great opening
of ironwood trees where sun
spreads across the morning sky,
I abandon trail, clumping over rocks
and foot falls hidden in tall grass

I take now the trail bulls plod, along the ocean,
to the dry bed that flows only in wildest storm,
carrying cars from road to ocean grave

I walk out at dawn
Down the rough pasture
Searching for the present moment
But I'm more in reminding
and clouds of thoughts
than present when the sea
strikes the rocks
Thurump!

An engine ignites
inside me, that for a time
turns grass green, making
every rock and bump
soft down for my foot

Entering the Pastures

In which I discover that my path to Leho'ula, and to my spiritual practice, is apparently blocked by developers, by threats to the environment, and I am urged by a descendant of ali'i to save the land.

Hoʻolae, a chief: *"When my son wanted Wananalua, I knew he wanted it for war. We have had enough wars along this coast. We fought for pastures of peace, where the spiritual work of Hāna could be accomplished. Make this the last battle."*

Arrgh. Usually Sunday is something special: We climb waterfalls; we scramble over rocks in lush valleys, tramping on flowers and leaves; we take the gentle path to Lehoʻula. Today, however, just a quick walk and back to work, and I am angry!

Usually, I feel flush with the fullness of my life. Today it feels chopped into little pieces, and scattered. The rage I feel scratches and crawls along the surface of my skin.

Today, I am choosing to take care of some business and it feels as if everywhere I go, there is a mattress awkwardly poised on my back. Bent over, bending down, a lump in my throat, my eyes closed to all experience, except longing to be somewhere I am not.

Later,

at last released

as I walk along the land . . .

A flock as small as hummingbirds
chirps delicate as thimbleberries
Tiny angels piping songs
along my way

A soft pillow of darkness
approaches, absorbing
the sea's sparkles in its milky black,
mournful to the mind, and unreachable

But look how the sun breaking through the morning clouds shines on the branches of palm and hala and ti. Crossing the pasture at Opuohina suddenly all is a flower, even the ocean, crashing and opening to embrace me. So intense the enormous beauty, I want to possess it.

"Imagine if I lived here! Here is where I shall plant my house.
This shall be mine forever. No one will take it away."

And I bind this beauty to me, with steel tension rods jutting out from my jaw, extending out from my arms to entrap the colors and the shapes and the freshness of the air—a flower closing over a fly.   The sun disappears behind thick clouds. All about me turns grey, and the beauty I thought to have captured disappears. I find instead only the steel wires and the rods, tension folding around me as I sink in the gloom.

This morning, loneliness and grief
Rumor has it that land
between us and the sea
is to be sold, and there is nothing
we can do.

Walking

through the fields and along the
shore of Leho‘ula, my fears twist into desires,
this world becomes a thrall of acquisitions. I don't
need a developer's fortune to rob my actions of their
dignity, to bind the sweeping sands to my mind; to
populate the fields with rich houses, with hedges,
with walls; to bring anxiety to the land—I
can do it in a moment with my
mind.

Just below my surface
I feel the volcanic fires
of Pele burning, ignited
by a rumor in my soul

Enormous powers reign
in these tropical mountains
where, behind hidden windows,
tiny eyes search the land
below, looking for a sale

How do I prevent
my tiny eyes
from responding?

This earth is a garden
Its aromas, its breezes
and its light: flavors of consciousness
Lava bridges from another world
to the one where we are meant to live

What if consciousness
itself rumbles along
the ocean floor?

What if this lava soil and its garden
are seeded with imagination?

How much then does it become worth,
this earth?

What if every change, each element,
each object, each nuance, glitters
with a divine light?

Worth our very lives? Every ounce
and every inch of them—
A price beyond measure

What if it is God himself
with whom we walk,
upon whom we rest
on these grassy hills?

Incomprehensible to those
who want to put boxes
on the grounds of paradise

How by slow and steady thought
We bind our spirits into knots.

I'm the one in agony
    it's not them
it's not their problem
they're not suffering

When I live in the land
of who I think I should be
even if only for a moment
even if only for tomorrow

I feel sick with disease
I feel ashamed
I feel as if my life is being blown back
I feel alone on black sand in a chill wind
that stretches for a thousand miles
and blows for ten thousand years
I feel like crawling into the dark shadow of a leaf

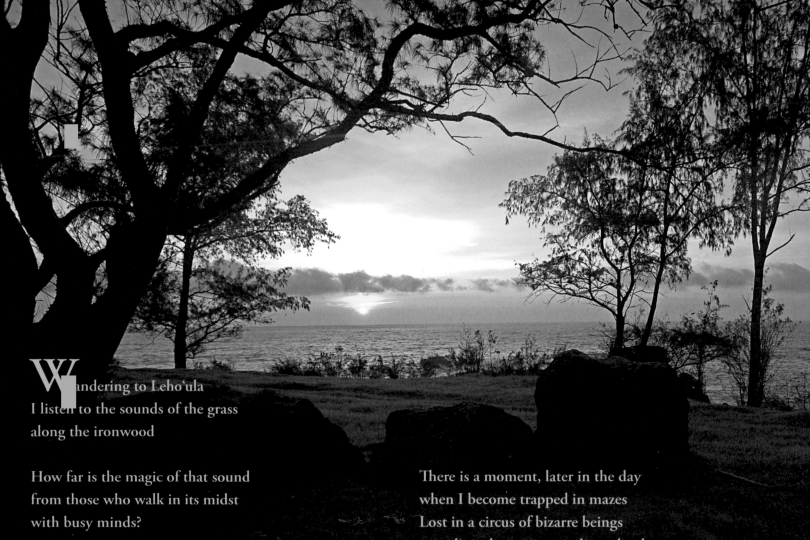

W andering to Lehoʻula
I listen to the sounds of the grass
along the ironwood

How far is the magic of that sound
from those who walk in its midst
with busy minds?

Who will weave its music and its aromas
around them, striding out upon the hills
like spirit warriors

calling from hill to hill
from island to island
to save this distant land?

There is a moment, later in the day
when I become trapped in mazes
Lost in a circus of bizarre beings
crowding about me on solitary land
And it is impossible to see the grass on which I walk
Impossible to feel clumps of earth under my feet

Until something shifts
And I become eager
to move with them

I have used my words as flailing torch
to sear others with my shame
But look!
It's not the stories; it's the fire that is real
It is the face of God, this fire
until, all burned away
I see myself

Such a tortured war we live in
with just these fragments of ourselves and others remaining
rather than how, free of time and space
we are the whirling winds where light comes from
and the sources of the singing
that arises from the ocean to the sky

Instead, hidden under such reasonable garb,
we make our spiritual reasons for war
for deceit for murder for fraud for theft for divorce
or for ripping up a pasture
that runs down from the mountain to the sea
as if it were a whale

Only the inner pasture is quiet
Only where birds chirp inside is alive

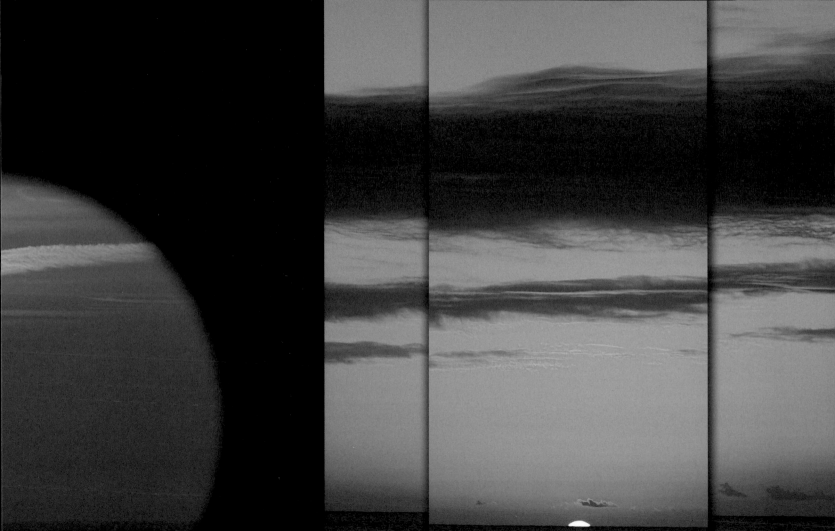

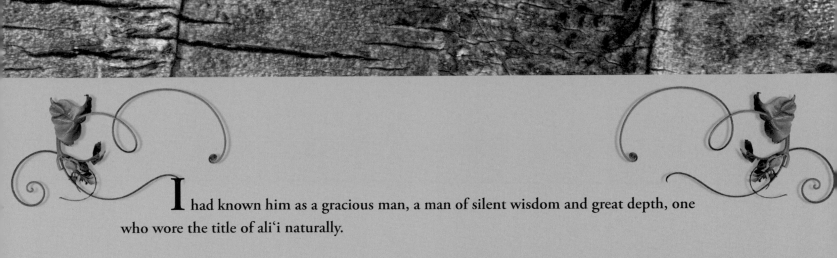

I had known him as a gracious man, a man of silent wisdom and great depth, one who wore the title of aliʻi naturally.

"You must stop this," he said as I told him of the sales of the land. "You must stop this," he bellowed. I marveled and imagined, as the voice echoed through the phone line, that it was not the voice of my friend, but the voice of Hawaiian ancestors. "You must stop this," he chanted. "It is your destiny! It is your destiny." I hung up the phone, shaken, honored, awed. What was this old man who had yelled at me over the phone? Who did he think he was? How could I do anything? I had no one's respect. I did not hold reins of power.

Each time we met, without fail, he would draw me aside and say,
"Live in Aloha, the message of Hawaii is Aloha.
It's our message to the world."
But shouldn't we fight? Isn't there a battle?
"Your greatest weapon is Aloha."

There is a villainous darkness to development.
Roads and walls and street lamps and hedges
block the spirit of the ocean, obscure its view,
prevent it from wandering up through the fields
through car windows and the windows of our eyes
into the hearts of the people of Hāna and its visitors.
House, hedge and wall come to possess our spirits,
drawing them away from the ʻāina to ghoulish gossip
and fearful thought.

But the spirit of Hāna
despite the darkness of our souls
carries through waving grasses and its birds,
bringing music of the moment
down the coast, delivering the present
to my ear again and again as the wind rushes by

In slanting blades
wet light
falls

On my left
ocean carves
cliff

On my right
a bull!
watches

In the middle
nothing
but the lush green grass

of Hāna

THE SPIRIT OF THE SKY

A little squiggle rises from the sea at the edge of the sky
A fingerful of green light
wriggles out of the ocean
bursts into a flaming orange globe
and sits upon the water like a throne

Thoughts like broken breezes come and go
Their moods race along the wild landscape
through stream beds
Falling like egrets
Bursting through soil
Dissolving like dew

No Trespassing

I

I wander lost on the land, so great is my grief
I cannot bear what might be done to Lehoʻula
What will happen to Ka iwi o Pele?
What are these clouds, these hedges and these walls
doing in the free pathways of my mind?

II

I see the sun rise as it did
before the ancestors
I hear the first birds of morning
thread their tune through the crashing waves
Called away from a busy life
I follow the breezes, through pastures
Through wild gardens of the gods along the sea

I walk alone
Whispering to the land with each breath
Speaking its language
Listening for an answer
I must look like a ghost dancing
as I caress the air
asking for its blessing

Oh my God . . .
Do I see Lehoʻula in bed with the Developers?
Is this the meaning of Pele, ravished by the god of the pigs?

Lehoʻula with her wild matted hair
like roots hanging from Pele's bones
down to the tawny shore

After the storm

The cries of birds on all sides
I stride the ocean road
Deep in feeling
Alert to every sensation

Arrayed across the clouds
like a band of angels
a hundred snowy egrets
fall upon black bulls

Pele and Her Friends

In which Pele, the goddess of fire and the volcano; Kuʻulakai, the god of the fish; his son Aiʻai; Kamapuaʻa, the god of the pigs; and St. Francis all give encouragement, as I pursue my spiritual quest.

Ku'ulakai, God of the Fish

Waking up, I see an enormous man. At first I think he's a bear or a bull standing on the ocean. It looks as if the ocean waters have receded and he is diving in, then standing up, shaking the water off his body—a huge square jaw, a gleam in his eye and a smile on his face.

He dives in. I half expect to see him come out with a fish between his teeth. He seems to be hauling something like a net, but when he turns and grins at me I realize he has been hauling my spirit up from the ocean floor. What for, I wonder?—this man, whose body glistens in the sun, whose surface seems to be of hair, of fur, of mud, of water, and then the smoothest skin, this big bear, fish of a man, with his huge head and square-jawed grin. What is he doing with my soul?

First Ku'ulakai, then his son Ai'ai—
Who alone survived the attack of the chiefs
Who killed the giant eel—
Tamed the chaotic ocean
Placing fishponds along
the coasts of all Hawaii

They spoke words of eternity to me
in their human forms
At 'Aleamai
Near the base of Ka iwi o Pele
Above the bay
At Leho'ula

AI'AI   "Sometimes you have to hide out
Sometimes you have to lay low
But create. Listen to me. Create!
Look at what we did, Ku'ulakai and I
At Leho'ula and Haneo'o—the fishponds
Raised the spirits of our people
Though they cost my father his life

Make your mark in Hāna
Rise against unjust powers
as we rose above the chaos

of the sea."

I saw St. Francis with Aiʻai
I thought I heard them speak
I felt the words of Francis
course along my cheek

Oh that they stay
out of the path
of the river of fire
and Peleʻs wrath

Hand in hand
They walked the land
Their words fell
like ocean mist

I saw Aiʻai and Francis
and felt them in my feet,
each grain of glistening sand
insisting that we meet

43

PIG GOD
KAMAPUAʻA
Then Kamapuaʻa, god of the pigs
greeted me with a smile
that moved like a wave
from his face to my own
then back, blossoming
into a big belly laugh
"Ha, Ha, Ha! Hā-na.

Hey boy, for years I've seen you walking
up and down the beach at Lehoʻula.
What are you doing there?"

I'm trying to capture moments.

"Ah, so you're a hunter too."

Each moment must be met,
Spoken, brought to life.
Not one can be lost.

It's my practice to be with the roots of life
With the grasses—nameless
With the sand rolling up from the sea

The self's thoughts are weeds to pick
Ha! Here's one: That's a flower!
Would you like it?"

"Ha, Ha, Ha! Hā-na means the breath of spirit and its work.
Do your work. Master what you do. Bring the land back to the people.
But—listen kid, you want my advice—against the great powers, even Pele, you
have to love. Love what feeds you, love your resources, love your fire, love what
challenges you, love your enemies—I love pigs man—but love!"

46

Encouraged as I was by these encounters
the one I longed for most remained
but a melody floating on distant air

I cannot wander far from Lehoʻula
She calls me back to her crescent beach
and the crumbling cliffs of Ka iwi o Pele

How many mornings sitting under the banyan
and the coconut palm do I hear her call
A lover that's been lost, her trees fallen
her sands washed out, her pavilion gone?

How many nights have I mourned her spirit
Feared for her land?

(I will haunt these shores of Lehoʻula
Ocean waters crashing over red bones.)

How long can Pele stay silent?

Once ravished here by the god of pigs
How long now will she allow
the ravishing of her land?

PELE Goddess of Fire

"I am here.
Why do you come to visit me?
In this time?

In this darkness?"

My life is not complete without your sacred fire.   I was married here — in the fire pit, strewn with rose petals, blessed by the sweet sounds of Kāleo's ukulele.   You have been gracious to me for all these years and to my friends in Hāna, but now I am fearful for your land and for your fire.

"You come to the foot of my sacred hill
as a blessing to the land
You are part of my family now
For I am about the fiery opening of the heart
Hearts that won't open, I burn.

I know you grieve, so grieve—the river of grief is the song that was paradise—but from your grieving passion create new land: CREATE A SONG SO STRONG THAT PEOPLE CAN WALK ON IT.   Grieve, but enter your grief, not lost in thought.   Each thought is like a new building scarring the land, but the river of fire, the river of grief is the breath of life.

Breathe with breath of fire
Walk the warrior's step
Woo each spirit you meet
with the heart of a poet
a lover, a mother

All the things you thought dead
will come alive, things beyond
your dreams, so fertile this place
This land, so wise its mana

Breathe, breathe into the land

Haven't you noticed, once you enter the garden
Nothing happens—not rain, not wind, not ocean's roar
Not the rising of the sun from the ocean floor
Not your worries, not even your suffering
But there's a spark of divinity to it

It's as if God herself willed it all to happen
It's as if, when you choose to be present
You enter God's realm, and there's no causality
It's just what is, and it flows through your veins
Like fire

If you stop being present, everything hardens,
Becomes black, brittle. Once you leave the fire
It takes tens of thousands of days, billions of moments
For the workings of the sun, for the wind and rain
For the wild song of the ocean to break you down
To call you back. To fill you so full of life
that green plants burst through your skin."

But what happens when I go back? When I leave the garden?

"Once you've entered, how can you leave the garden?"

But what happens if they take the garden away?

"Where is the garden?
Is not the garden in each moment
and in your skin?

Look, I left Maui after I was ravished
by the god of the pigs. I was devastated.
I loved that guy.

Things change, sometimes for the worse.
Sometimes it's tragic.
Sometimes a whole people gets lost
Sometimes your only child
It's what you do with that loss that counts.
Sometimes, you have to fight."

Nervous, agitated, insecure in Pele's presence I mutter
I would like to swim
as far as the ancient ones
To be with the fire of the sun
as it rises
from the ocean's bed

"You must imagine it
It is the place you come alive
each morning as you walk
the fragrant land, each fragile
moment billowing in the wind

You must bring the spark
of that moment inside

For each yearning, each longing
you cling to is a curtain across
your world–the rich man's
hedge dividing the limitless sky."

Pele continued:
"Like the greatest fire, the greatest wisdom often comes
from the smallest spark. There! That's it. Touch it. There!
Your fragility, your most vulnerable place.

You know, I once burned from a broken heart so piteously
and lost myself so totally that in a moment nothing but fire existed.
A moment later my heart opened, and what had been excruciating
became joyous, filled with profound music.

When I left it was as if I had pulled from the fire of ego its dying embers:
My world became quiet. What was once obscured by flames
of attachment was no longer hidden.

Ho! Set yourself on fire, my boy,
so you can burn yourself up!"

So much more to me was said
by Pele, Aiʻai, Kuʻulakai
and even more by the way the wind each day would take me in its arms,
or by the bellow of the bulls. The crashing ocean
came like a lullaby into my heart,
breaking the hold of the telephone
of the dollar
asking me to listen to the land
to find riches only in my heart
and in each moment
even when the fires of Pele's vengeance
and her fears burned most fiercely
for it was then, I came to learn
that everything I knew was coming to its end

Searching for Lehoʻula

In which I get down to business, doing my spiritual practice along the beach of Lehoʻula, and in which it becomes clear that the ancient Lehoʻula is none other than the present moment that I yearn for.

Leho'ula lies scattered in her sands,
Hidden in her dark caves
Lost in her waters

How can I call her forth?

There is a stand of trees, as thick as iron that we call self, profit, wisdom, love, truth.
Sometimes I can't see beyond it. This stand obscures my sight and all that might reveal itself.
It's as though I've been lost in the tresses of Leho'ula's veil, stumbling through her thousand
years of sleep, looking for new eyes with which to see her.

Oh Lehoʻula, shining spirit of our souls
Each day I come to your shore
I walk beneath your ancient leaves
Welcoming me to the feast of moments

I sit on the edge of the earth
Seawater lapping at my toes
Sand under my butt
Cross-legged in meditation
Only to lose myself in endless worry

But each time I come back to my breath
Everything falls into place

A door has closed
A door has opened

I hear a hidden waterfall
in every breath
Lush beside my heart

SEARCHING THE SEA FOR A MOMENT OF TIME

I catch so many moments
of guilt, of fear, of shame
as I walk across the sand

A warrior catching arrows
of delight
I place them in my quiver
and watch the waters
Searching for my prey

Fierce in silent meditation
A tiny cinder cone
rolling down the beach
startles me

How many canyons
and crevices
can the wind find

as it winds
its silken scarf
about me?

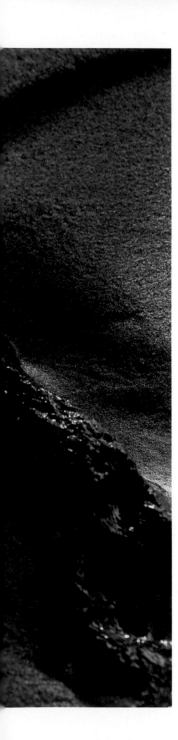

I keep wrestling with how to stay present
with these leaves, strewn upon the beach

How can I not lose myself in their beauty?

Then I realize it's something inside me, haunted,
Looking for a place of rest, something yearning
Something not dreamed through in the night
Something that has taken my morning vitality
to leap with restless anxiety
Anywhere it wants, anywhere but here

Gripped by unknown concerns
I'm lost in lethargy's sorrow
Yet even when my heart
is breaking, there is a steady
surface in the crumpled sand
beneath my feet

No matter how I try to stay present
Free from the taint of self
In the tiniest of thoughts
Hidden in the shadows
Beneath the black lava rocks
Like a crab, I rise
Hauling past and future
from the sand, and dump
them sprawling on the shore

SITTING MEDITATION THIS MORNING

My mind is tossed, scattered
Like waves on rocks

Thoughtlessly
upon awakening
I crush a little bug
on my poem

I watch the foam pull back
across the sloping sands
Lines of snow falling, sorrowful

What night of dalliance
left these leaves
languorous on the sand?

There is freedom
in every footfall
But you must feel
every footfall
to find it

As I was walking
Right in front of my eyes
The ocean
Sweeping beachward across my feet
With shreds of bark and leaf
Left lines of poetry, freshly turned
Then swept them away.

Hauling Poems up from the Ocean Floor or A Poet's View of a Poem

The way the waters of a wave are absorbed into sand
So a poem starts—wet with the smell of ocean

Over time its lines, set down,
are absorbed into the page

The poem, dried, no longer
has quite its original flavor

But soon takes life and speaks
from the rains, the rivers, the veins
All the liquid senses of the imagination

I

I sit in the shade of tree-limb and cloud
watching the tongue
of ocean lick the shore

II

Draping my body
like a tent

Under the ancient tree
I sit in silence

Till the ocean
Tells me who I am

NUI NUI   All of the bark and the leaf
of the beach
are gone

Only the soft
white rain
remains

67

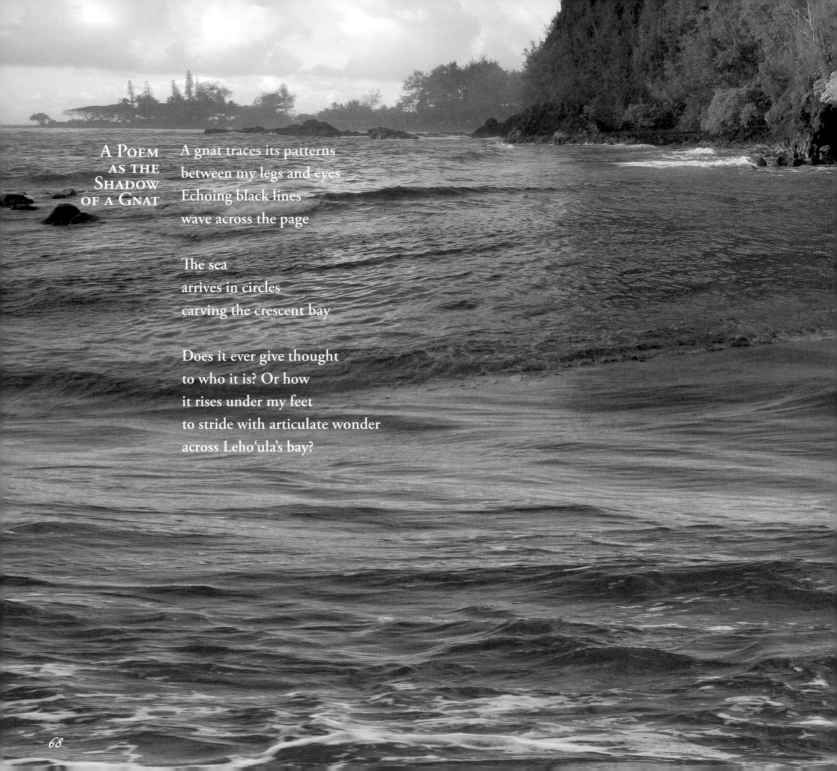

A POEM AS THE SHADOW OF A GNAT

A gnat traces its patterns
between my legs and eyes
Echoing black lines
wave across the page

The sea
arrives in circles
carving the crescent bay

Does it ever give thought
to who it is? Or how
it rises under my feet
to stride with articulate wonder
across Leho'ula's bay?

It's noisy at Lehoʻula
The ocean never stops talking
It's like someone you know very well
who always says the same thing
You don't really have to listen
Or so you think

Some strangers in shorts and bikini
have found their way to my walk.
I am nervous with these polished visitors
as wary in my rags of tai chi
as they must be of me
on this isolated beach
where Pele, the goddess of fire
was ravished by the god of the pigs

Sitting scared on the beach

There's no lurking danger
Not the ocean
Not strangers

It's only me
Sitting on the edge of the sea
Growing smaller

Not like when the ocean and sky swallow you up
Not like when the wind wraps you in its vanishing scarf
Not like when you enter the roar of the rocks

There you become a nothing that is everything
Here, I keep shrinking smaller and smaller

What a surprise, then, to hear Leho'ula
Sitting on this wet rock
Emerging from the darkness of the ocean's roar

Losing myself in her sacred sound
It's as if I sit on the sea itself
At the moment of creation

'Ālau sits, a lion
upon the sparkles of the sea

But for me
Before the day started
Fear in the flutter of a leaf

Now winds rush through my body

A mystery
Nothing but sparkles of the sea

Sometimes you just can't learn much
from the sea at Leho'ula

For instance
The sea rushes away
Washing stones over my feet
Always so busy, yet never getting anywhere

I'd kind of like to not get anywhere myself
I just don't want to be so damn busy about it

It's been a dark and cloudy day
My mind has stormed along the shores of Lehoʻula
I feel the sun's warm bite on my neck
A brilliant blue sky lights the towering cliffs
of Ka iwi o Pele

Watching a new wave wash over my toes
It reaches for the farthest shore
and falls back

I think of Aiʻai's father
Every day adding knowledge to his life
Adding volumes to his shelves

Only to fall back, one sudden day,
to the sea of his being
Only the faintest trace
of his teachings
remaining

In the sand

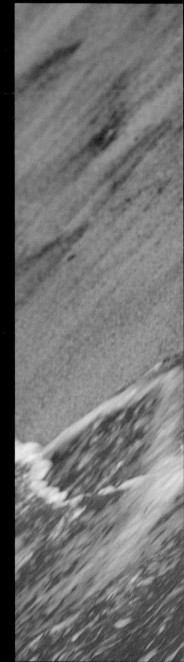

For a moment
The ocean crashed against a rock
Spray rose into the sky
Masking the sun
A veil of water drawn between us

Last night
I rose in the dark
No one was there
Just the feeling
of skin and soft fingers
Rubbing along the caverns
of grape-like eyes

Tell me
Who is this I
This veil of water
Racing against the sun?

The spirit of Lehoʻula keeps calling me
And yet, as a poet I am poverty stricken
I have spent so many days under her arbors
Walking her crescent beach
Searching for moments in the sand
And all I have are these few lines

A bird cries out, raucous
That bird, such a chorus
in the golden light
after the storm

Sand races through my hair
Closed-eyed in meditation
The wind must have blown

me away

At last Leho'ula reveals herself, an 'īwī, a beautiful young woman, a goddess of wisdom and of all times. Leho'ula and I lose ourselves in passionate embrace, spat with each other, reconcile, and part as true lovers. Leho'ula passes on her teachings and promises to live in my song.

I have always imagined Lehoʻula
as a woman along whose skirt
I was graced to walk

At last I see her
Wading across waves
On the sands of Lehoʻula

Moving closer, she speaks
"In hiding we meet across barbed wire
Pulled through pastures of bulls
Over No Trespassing signs

I hear your breath as I sleep
I am startled by your songs
Secretly I steam your glasses

Your chants shake me into the depths
    of my being
Your warm body and beating heart curl
along the curl of my cove
Your fingers and toes
reach into my soft white foam

Yet you are not the only one who comes
The pastures of Wananalua are grieving
The snowy egrets and the great black bulls
Haleakalā herself quakes and groans
and Pele, Aiʻai, Kuʻulakai

The trees of Ka iwi o Pele fall on my sands
My caves collapse
Great boulders crash to the ground

Time is urgent
From Kaʻuiki to Makaalae, developers
have spotted the heroic ancient lands
The spiritual gardens
Seeing them only as bits of flesh
To be snatched and shaken and tossed in the wind
To be devoured and transformed
     into rich mans' bones
Their walls, their hedges and their homes."

I don't think I understood a word of what she said, so stunned was I to see her. As she spoke it seemed the land was becoming human. The smallest grain of sand sparkled with life. The cliffs of Ka iwi o Pele gently shook into Kamapua'a's bold form, each tree a warrior, guarding the land, calling its warning out to all Hawaii. Even the clouds seemed to sing. The sun burst forth godlike, and the air lifted the earth up in its warm embrace.

On ʻĀlau, the great god Maui stands, hauling his islands up from the sea. Aiʻai and Kuʻulakai, like dolphins, leap from the ocean to dance through the sky with the ʻiwi Lehoʻula. Standing tall, they hold the long sandy tresses of Lehoʻula's veil as she sails across the bay. Pele gathers her cloak around the sun, shining its light on her friends. The words of Lehoʻula bleed from her dress, they echo in the hills, stirring the breezes.

Here on the beach of Lehoʻula, leaning on my knapsack, feeling the words of the wind, I watch the passionate heart of the ocean cascading toward my feet and listen to the celebrations of the birds of wonder crying out the rising of the sun.

Changing in each moment, a giant 'iwi, a snowy
egret, a gracious woman walking along the sands,
Leho'ula, a great gasp of wonder, breaks each element
into something else. The sparkles in the sand become
stars swirling around me. My feet lose their steadiness
and I fall into a cloudy swirling darkness. I become a
flaming spirit falling through the air, through the water,
no body, just breathing, breathing, breathing, breathing.
For the longest time, no stories. Just Leho'ula, breathing
beneath me and the sounds of the ocean crashing, and
the cries of the 'iwi.

Like a crab, my darling
races from the onslaught
of ocean and pokes me
with her claws

"Wake up at once," she whispers.

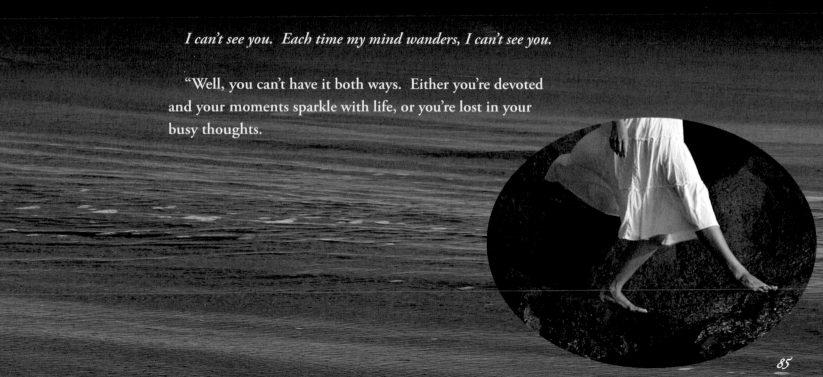

You think you're so special coming to see me, but you're like so many other men. You pay no attention, you fall asleep, you come, you go. You get pulled to business to 'do' things. You don't even see what's here!" Leho'ula cried out, fearless, radiantly beautiful, her delicate white wings dazzling in the sun.

I can't see you. Each time my mind wanders, I can't see you.

"Well, you can't have it both ways. Either you're devoted and your moments sparkle with life, or you're lost in your busy thoughts.

Each moment is an angel, an ancestor, a kupuna, your only child. Think of each moment as your darling, whispering songs of joy and songs of woe into your ears. Each moment is a world, already breathing.

You spend a fortune to discover life on one of Saturn's moons
but you don't know what life is
How could you possibly think you could discover
life on another planet
when you haven't discovered it inside yourself
How it arises, fresh inside, how it feels
and how it heals
The world is inside out
It's not physics
You are the course of study
Don't fall into the sleep of thought
What you want and what you think
is so much less than who you are
Find out who you are!

You walk outside of yourself like a ghost, not a spirit,
onto the surfaces of a world that disappears in a moment.
Each moment is treacherous, like a lover on her deathbed
This world is wild and unknowable, nimble and spontaneous
It's not what you think.

Your thoughts are the shroud I've been hiding in
for a thousand years. No more!
They hide the truth of life itself
It's all in the moments. Rescue them!
The world is inside out

Watch the breath, the Hā of Hāna, day and night
The angels of the earth, the ones that sing along
the shores of Wananalua on down to Ka iwi o Pele

They're inside you
They're in your sensations
They're in your breath
They're calling you

Do you think they have no meaning?"

You say the world is inside out
But deep inside there are no developers
There is no aliʻi. Pele herself is passing away
What can I do with that?

"What you think of as doing is merely scheming
If you are still in the world of doing
you have not understood your own breath."

Then she rises
passing through me
like wind blown rain.

But, is it over? Is all lost?

"I have given up the ends you seek
My sands are not of this world.
Are yours?"

But look what I've done to find you
Walking endlessly along your shores
Till I forget who I am
How do I go back?

"You're born into a world
(Get food, clothing, shelter)
But you are meant to live
A spirit life

This world is just a garb
you wear. Give it its due
but no more

Stand against walls, hedges, houses
but if you find yourself on these skirts,
these sloping sands and you can't see
Return to my caves
Take rest on my shores

There is no way into truth
other than the clear-seeing moment
None at all

Except for the moment
The earth is merely a map
But enter the moment
and the earth becomes real

89

Leho'ula: "I have been sleeping for the longest time but now I am awake
I have dreamed, wild dreams of Pele, of Maui, of the sun
and of the old days, before the betrayal
Before there was a world of stories
and their kapu, the world of authority
covering us like a coffin
Let me tell you a story

It was a beautiful day
I was to be married on this beach
From all the islands people came, equal on my shores
The taro farmer and the pig hunter and the hale builders and 'opihi gatherers
And their uncles and aunties and their little ones
For all things were in balance, the inner life was rich in vision
And its feast was rich, and the cloth was pounded fine

Hundreds came, from all the islands to celebrate
our marriage, bearing aloha in their flowers and feathers
Their hula and their chants—but it was a trap, and the blood
of my lover was shed by a traitor's song that started
a thousand years of war along this shore

So I went inside
Into the sands
Into the wind
Into the light

And remained hidden
Till one returned
with true love
in his heart

From that time
People lived for the bitter rind of the fruit
Robbed by envy of the gift of moments
They created a world of authority
and filled it with stories of themselves

They broke my marriage, they murdered my
    betrothed
But I learned to love them
Not for what they did, but for who they are
when they live in their own forgiveness
who they become in a world of blessing

You must know how this world falls apart
Its chaos—and how it flourishes
(which are the same thing)
before your actions have meaning

Even then, that which has meaning for you
may for the world be like placing a fishpond
too deep in the sea

Inside each of us a universe
as large as the universe itself
Eight billion universes
just among human beings
not to mention the dolphins and the birds
the pueo, the 'iwi, every developer
A universe of wonder inside themselves

Oppose the developers, sure
Awaken them, better still
But respect that universe
so much greater
than the plot of land they wish to conquer

Bring aloha to their universe
Love them as you have loved me
That is the way to make Hāna free

We live in a universe of moments
Not of atoms, not of particles or thoughts
A universe of living moments."

   *Wait a minute. You're talking about two worlds,
you're talking about forgiving the developers and
loving them and then you're jumping into another
place, another universe. I don't get it. There's
something missing.*

"Right there! Look at the wall you put between the
    ocean and the sky
Mother Earth is a living spirit—we rest in her being
Each moment born, each moment dying. Trust her.

The world is not broken by your darkness nor can it
    be manipulated by your light
All these days it was only you who blocked the
    ancient ways.
But you have done the work, you have sung the
    song.

Life itself is the miracle
Time to hoist your sails
The wind is with you!"

Ah…

"My long night of slumber is over
I will sleep in the sands no longer
Take me now into the coves of your heart
Take me within the softest of your senses
Feel my life inside yours, stretching out
over the pastures of Hāna, sloping down
to the sea

In the breath of your song I will be bold
I will let my fountains rush forth
and cry out across the mourning hills
Calling from island to island
to keep Hāna free."

"Take comfort now, you sacred sands
I will no longer weep for you
Take comfort now
Take comfort now
Find rest within me while I act."

Lehoʻula flies up into the sky
  and over the hills
from Makaalae to Wananalua
  chanting
"I live inside your song."

At last I surrender to the wind
All earth's structures are crumbling
All its thoughts
Like the cliffs of Ka iwi o Pele
Falling to Leho'ula's shore

Walking Back

In which I grieve Leho'ula's passing, celebrate my new understanding and begin to integrate my spiritual practice with my daily life.

Returning home, I am sand
dropping through a sieve
Ocean water falling
from flapping wings
Self all gone

I pass through changing moments
As if they were grasses
Whispering along the shore

I rise, a great river rushing
from my spine, upward
and outward into oceans
of moments of time

It's in the gardens of the wind and the wild ocean
I do the work. I enter a paradise
Only to discover it's not
When I confuse the vitality
        of changing moments
with anxiety or death

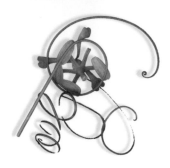

Walking along the cliffs from Lehoʻula to Wananalua
I hear Lehoʻula's voice cry out across the mourning hills

How in love I am with all its sensations
I want to stay till I've plumbed its mystery
But as I go along, everything passes
One soft footstep after another
One fickle moment of cloud
changes everything

Now I see
What I want to know
is not how things stay
But how they
Come and how they go

I live in the celebration of Lehoʻula
and mourn her at the same time
Mourn her passions
Mourn her passing
as if she has actually died
As if her song were ended

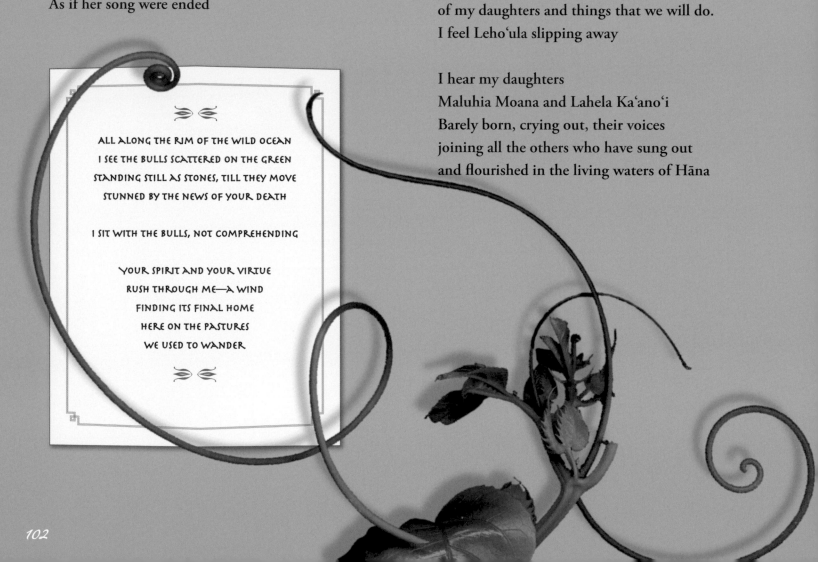

ALL ALONG THE RIM OF THE WILD OCEAN
I SEE THE BULLS SCATTERED ON THE GREEN
STANDING STILL AS STONES, TILL THEY MOVE
STUNNED BY THE NEWS OF YOUR DEATH

I SIT WITH THE BULLS, NOT COMPREHENDING

YOUR SPIRIT AND YOUR VIRTUE
RUSH THROUGH ME—A WIND
FINDING ITS FINAL HOME
HERE ON THE PASTURES
WE USED TO WANDER

Walking back, filled already with thoughts
of my daughters and things that we will do.
I feel Lehoʻula slipping away

I hear my daughters
Maluhia Moana and Lahela Kaʻanoʻi
Barely born, crying out, their voices
joining all the others who have sung out
and flourished in the living waters of Hāna

Meeting moments at Leho‘ula
In the long hours of the day
In the rainy season
In all your years

The world turns inside out
And the deep peace within
Spreads across the landscape
Across the wild ocean
Across every changing moment

The world keeps shifting
And the inner peace keeps arising
It's like the world keeps getting anxious
Keeps being born and dying
And with what you have deep inside
You keep bringing it to rest

You might call it spiritual work
Or you might call it suffering
transformed into wisdom
I like to call it the song of Hāna.

Glossary

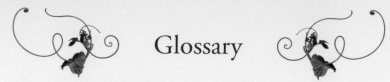

ahupua'a	Land division usually extending from the uplands to the sea, so called because the boundary was marked by a heap (ahu) of stones surmounted by an image of a pig (pua'a).
Ai'ai	Son of Ku'ulakai.
'āina	Land, earth.
'Ālau	Island off the Hāna coast.
'Aleamai	Location in Hāna, near Leho'ula.
ali'i	Chief, ruler, monarch, nobility.
aloha	Greeting, affection, kindness, love.
hala	The pandanus or screw pine.
hale	House, building, lodge.
Haleakalā	Mountain above Hāna with dormant volcano; highest peak on Maui.
Hāna	1. "Spiritual work," 2. a town and district in East Maui.
Haneo'o	Place name of early fish pond in Hāna, near Leho'ula.
Ho'olae	Maui chief, 19th century.
'iwi	1. Var. of 'i'iwi, a bird. 2. Reddish.
kahuna	Expert in any profession, priest. Kāhuna, plural of kahuna.
ka'ano'i	The desired one.
Ka iwi o Pele	"The bone of Pele," hill above Leho'ula.
Kāleo	Musician in Hāna.
Kamapua'a	The god of the pigs.
kapu	Taboo, prohibition; sacredness, no trespassing, keep out.
Ka'uiki	Head, point, hill, and lighthouse, Hāna, Maui.
Kīpahulu	Place near Hāna and Oheo gulch.
kupuna	Grandparent, ancestor, relative or close friend of the grandparent's generation, grandaunt, granduncle. Kūpuna, plural of kupuna.
Ku'ulakai	God of the fish. Father of Ai'ai.
Lahela	Rachel.
Leho'ula	Beach in Hāna and the rare and highly prized red cowry shell.
Makaalae	Place in Hāna, beyond Hamoa.
Maluhia	Peace, quiet, security, tranquility, serenity. The deep peace that arises in religious ceremony.
mana	Supernatural or divine power or spirit.
Mauna Kea	The highest mountain on the Big Island of Hawaii, snow mountain.
mele	Song, anthem, or chant of any kind; poem.
Moana	Ocean, open sea.
nui nui	Soft, white rain.
'opihi	Limpets – marine mollusks having tent shaped shells and adhering to rocks of tidal areas.
Opuohina	Small, beautiful bay between Ka'uiki and Leho'ula.
Pele	Volcano goddess.
pueo	Hawaiian short-eared owl.
ti	A woody plant in the lily family.
Waipama	A coastal area between Kauiki and Opuohina.
Wananalua	Pasture and coastal area including much of Hāna town.

Organizations Supporting Hāna

The following organizations support Hāna in many ways: its people, its culture, the preservation of its land. I am certain the list is incomplete. If by chance I have left you out, please let me know for the next edition of **A Song for Hāna & the Spirit of Leho'ula**.

Ala Kukui
Alu Like
East Maui Taro Festival
E.F. Schumacher Society
Hale Hulu Mamo
Hāna Arts
Hāna Canoe Club
Hāna Community Association
Hāna Community Health Center
Hāna Cultural Center
Hāna 'Ohana
Hāna Youth Center

Hui No Ke Olo Pono
Kahanu Gardens
Kipahulu 'Ohana
Kukulu Kumuhana
Maka Hāna Ka 'Ike
Maui Coastal Land Trust
Maui Tomorrow
Na Mamo o Mu'olea
Nature Conservancy
'Ohana Makamae Inc.
Sierra Club
Queen Liliuokalani Childrens Center

People Who Have Contributed

The following people inspired, supported, or encouraged me. I thank you all.

Dawn Lono, a truly inspiring leader and member of the Hāna community. One who loves Hāna and its people beyond measure. One who has understood in the deepest possible way, the connection between the sacred land and its people.

Joanne Fanning, who contributed her artistry to the scans of Hawaiian plants, who has passionately supported efforts to protect the land, and who has done so much for me and my family over the years.

Maryellen Grady, who, while keeping my office going and organizing the early stages of Serenity Point Press, has read and typed every iteration of *A Song for Hāna* from its first haiku. Thank you for keeping me sane.

Frank Siteman, who never doubted my ability to photograph the Hāna coast. Without your kind and persistent coaching, your inspired teaching, I would never have had the camera or Photoshop skills to deliver this book.

Tom Kinder, poet. Much thanks for your many careful readings of the poem, your thoughtful edits, but most of all for your large questions about the varying levels of meaning in the text and imagery.

Marc Zegans, who contributed a powerful final edit and confirmation. Thank you for your visionary insight, your comprehension, understanding, and your attention to the music of the line.

Drexel Ace. Thank you on so many fronts, and in particular for your fine ear as a poet, and your fine eye as a copy-editor.

Nadine Mazzola. Outside of my family, the greatest thanks goes to you, for living and breathing with the imagery of the book over the six months we took to bring it to production. Your sense of design and many skills contributed more than anything to the completion of the book. What I have appreciated most has been your infectious and inspired passion for the work throughout.

For my family, my wife and daughters, my father and brothers. Thanks most for your patience when I've been absent. My father, Gordon Kinder, introduced me many years ago to Kenny Brown, who completely changed my understanding of Hawaii, introducing me to the courage, nobility, and spiritual quality of its people, as well as to a sense of its world-wide mission and purpose. My mother, Cary Kinder, gave me the love of art, literature and a spiritual life. My wife, Kathy Lubar, has given so much to this work, including her many readings of it, contributing the ear and drama of a professional actor to so many pages and poems. Thank you for that, but most of all for your support, encouragement and love.

So many other people have contributed to this book. Many directly in their review of the poetry or the images, some without knowing it, by their creative spirit, through their love of Hāna, in the kindness of their being. Among those who have meant the most:

Ian Ballantyne

John Blumer Buell

Gertrude Boerner

Kenny Brown

Lesley Bruce

Patricia Cabellon

Rocky & Diedre Cimarusti

Justine Delfino

Coila Eade

Adam Freedman

Krista Fuglestad

Robin Gaffney

Susan Galvan

Emily Grady

Lisa Hamilton

Hilary Harts

Tim Heath

Bully Hoʻopai

Kema Kanakaole

Carol Kapu

Lisa Kristofferson

Leimamo Wahihākō-Lee

Erin Lindbergh

Carl & Rae Lindquist

Nancy Love

Phillippe Luzier

Loralee Machabee

Randy & Armine Medeiros

Richard Miller

Susie Miller

Kathryn Ellis Moore

Susan O'Connor

Richard Pasley

Jeannie Pechin

Pōhaku Lee

Dot & Chester Pua

Sally Reed

Helga Seibert

Francis Sinenci

Gaylord Stadshaug

Jane Alden Stevens

Marie Swift

Duke Walls

Lesley Wellman

Albert Zeman

I hope that I have remembered everyone. I *thank* you all.

SCOOPING THE MOON OUT OF THE BLUEBERRY SKY

Oh that I might leap up to the moon
To dance my delight upon the sky
So nimble is this thrill in my brain
Just from being alive

GEORGE KINDER is a poet, spiritual teacher, life planner, artist and photographer. He has been coming to Hāna since 1979, and makes his home in both Hāna and Massachusetts.

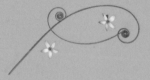

Help Save the Hāna Coast

'The Last Hawaiian Place'

There are many ways to help preserve the Hāna coast. Just as 50% of the profits from this book will be dedicated to helping preserve Hāna's coastline, so also will a percentage of the profits from the sale of photographs of the Hāna coast be contributed to organizations working to save the coastline, and/or preserve and support traditional Hawaiian culture.

Visit the Serenity Point Press website to:

- Order photographs
- Order books in quantity
- Order bumper stickers to save the Hāna coast
- Contribute directly to charitable organizations aiming to preserve the Hāna coast.

www.serenitypoint.org

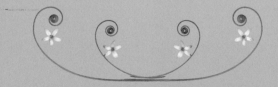